AMNESTY
(Poems)

Kemi Atanda Ilori

Universal Books

UNIVERSAL BOOKS
Holly Way
LEEDS
LS14 6NF

Published in the United Kingdom by Universal Books

www.universalbooksuk.co.uk

Information on this title:
www.universalbooksuk.co.uk/ilori

First published 1988 by the Association of Nigerian Authors (ANA), through Update Communications Limited, 51 Coker Road, Ilupeju, Nigeria

This edition printed in the United Kingdom
A catalogue record for this publication is available from the British Library

ISBN 978-1-910609-13-2 Paperback

Acknowledgement
Many thanks to my teachers, particularly, Professor Biodun Jeyifo, whose interest in my creative writings in those early years became the springboard for most of the poems in this volume.

I also acknowledge the shared foundry I found in the regular poetry reading sessions with my colleagues and students between 1983 and 1990.

As I read the poems in this volume again, I tried hard and overcame the urge to re-write some of them. Accordingly, apart from very slight amendments, I have left most of the poems undisturbed. New editions of some of the poems will be found in my newer collections.

Dedicated to the memory of my parents,
Tokunbo (1915-1974)
The iron forge and the kernel
and **Ebun** (1926-1988)
Daughter of the savannah
Who came to the forest
To breed her own offspring

and

For **Girlie**, my **Eja Osan** and the footsteps of dawn.

Contents

Poem	Page
The Poet's Eye	1
Scars of Our Previous Deaths	2
All They Want from Us	3
They Carry Within the Gloves	4
The Agents of Our Enemy	5
For the Decembrists	6
Coup	9
Barbiturates	11
Fugitive	13
Poems for Calico, the Dustman of Sabo	18
For Chief M.A. Fabunmi	22
Far from My Errant Selves	25
I Press from Leaf and Juice	28
Amnesty	29
Song	30
Isaac	31
Oh, Mamman!	33
In Memory of Dele Giwa	35
For Samora Machel	39

I Prowl the Understreams of Night   40

Masks   45

The House of Ageless Nod   50

Porcelain   52

Far Away from You   53

Pluck Me Like Leaf   57

Song of the Waistruff   60

Afterwards   62

New Year's Eve Sleuth   65

The Poet's Call   68

I Anoint My Eyes   70

Postscript   72

THE POET'S EYE

your eye is the evil we must combat
drench with the fumigant of a special decree

its lens magnifies the warts of State
the lepro in the linen of protocol

your eye: grand evil we must combat
pierce with the point of poisoned patronage

poet – your eye photographs our nakedness
fouls the labyrinth of our fortresses
your eye lifts the roof off our palaces
inveighs against the secrecy of our vaults
your eye hawks the death cries of the malcontent
rouses the tribune to revolt
your eye laminates the State
libels us in the presence of the people

poet, your eye is the blackmail we must combat
crush with the whet diplomatic pumice

WE are champions of abuse
of the sledgehammer-and-mattock oath
of power wrought like a wreath of manacles.

THE SCARS OF OUR PREVIOUS DEATHS

the scars of our previous deaths twitch
at the touch of iron rust
like carbuncles moistened by mist
earth's callous skin crusts
beneath the gloves of dew

come, o mask of Night
approach with your ultimate Silence
shut in the carapace of your soul

errors that must vanish
with the proof of dawn

from these kingdoms
a thousand witnesses unto self-death
when flesh keeps from bone
the windy secret of an obscure flea

errors that want the varnish
of dusk: the brittle of iron rust

from mysterious silence, half-carcases
of migrant worlds.

ALL THEY WANT FROM US

all they want from us is a testimony
of our death
the suicide we committed yesterday
on simple request

they are not interested in our anguish
our voices of indictment
at complacent perches

are we truly dead
are we smouldering in our tombs
are we at the portals of hell, singing
hymns at Lucifer's behest?

All they want from us is a testimony
Of our death
The suicide we committed yesterday
On simple request.

THEY CARRY WITHIN THE GLOVES

they carry within the gloves
of their innocence, earth's own

smitten soul: knife at centre-flesh
withdrawing from Truth's own flame

they keep from us their hangman's
gloves, the ominous innocence
of earth's own quintessence

o maid of the eyeless Night
mistress of horror in rites of rout
find from the soul's anguished squelch
the barren moist for the season's drought.

THE AGENTS OF OUR ENEMY

horror,
and night flees into the rafters
the masks have completed their old veneration
new men are bled from whitewashed tombs

the agents of our enemy
speak to us in coffee parlours
the paymaster wants a tête-à-tête
the spider spins its baft of ambush

we don't want to parley with our murderer
headghost of the mattock cult

out there our assassins wait
in the grey underclothes of dusk
their hit-list lit in the glare of glow worms

bring your tom-tom
headghost
the iron oath of the sledgehammer

armoured in the black cloth of labour
we await in mockery

the axe's angry descent.

FOR THE DECEMBRISTS
(Lagos, 1983)

1.
HAVING pissed into my seat
shift partner beyond the gathering pool
shift to the edge of the bench

where your unsoiled dress
can stay safe from stain

I have had dreams of the slaughter
in parliament
had dreams of bull crocodiles mating
in the cool shade of state chambers

shift, folk
shift your unsoiled seat to the edge
of the bench, extend your constituency
into the sharp margins of the dark forests

having pissed into my seat
leave me to fend for my friends
my friends imprisoned
in the vaults of state.

2.
the news reached us
while we were still naked
our long penises immersed in the sediment
of the village stream

we laughed then
halting the breeze with the foulness
of our mouths, clasping

in our rust-ridden palms
history's frantic sandpaper
the sponge of our numerous betrayals

we heard the capital was burning
that the fire brigade had given up
that the conflagration had spread to official quarters!

we laughed merrily
towelling our scarred bodies
with the ragged anthems and slogans
of the state, with the green-white-grin
frock of State House

3.
o, Minister, listen
we don't want the fatherland to burn
but what can we do in our nakedness
our long uncircumcised penises
immersed in muddy water?

the news reached us
while we were still thinking
of the cindered roots of being –

the pair of sandals
lying like limpid olive
in the sweltering porch of parliament.

COUP

(Lagos, 1985)

1.
it is recruits who man the guns
that keep the passage safe

all the officers need is shoot their boots
to power and provide
the raison d'être

where the carcase is big
the vultures are many
the scramble for the trophy

ends in a melee

oh, General, climb the platform again
inspect the guard of honour
take the 21-gun salute

from the awnings of our roof thatch
behind the faltering beams
of our reed gates

we watch this annual rite
of "army arrangement".

2.
let the medals keep up
the cannonade and the subaltern
the march-songs of the parade

in the cracks of the barracks
and the tumbling roofs of the city
in the weather-worn country
angst festers in the womb of time
and the terror of mass unrest

stalks the outskirts of Ribadu Road!

BARBITURATES

They sell us barbiturates
beneath the blanket of Night to halt
the raid in the eyes of men

They sell us hashish and amphetamine
- somnolent food for our angry veins –
to assist them in combatting

The fire in their summer roofs
new chimneys of liquor leap
into our sleep and casks of exotic spirits

Mask our callused dreams
Night is waiting for us beyond the hooded
pines, waiting for our bodies

In the sad sweat sleeves; encumbered
by misted rites, eyes drift into the torrid
knickers of Night

The half-asleep nature of half-men
everybody wants to know
what is wrong with the hungry crowds

Have they resigned to fate
to the long rope of suicide hanging
in the ceiling, to the coming

Of Xt. at the end of Time?

WE are far from suicide
and pagans before your skyward
riddles: we are Earth's children

The furnace in the sweaty womb
the thing that will explode
beneath the cloud face of our murderers' dreams.

FUGITIVE

1.
I want the deep silence of the abyss
the rest from the uproar in the cities

I want the deep moments of peace
not the strident voices of the past
challenging, questioning
upbraiding

It's enough – this season of self-torment
when abrasive ghosts of childhood
haunt the province of vision

I want silence
silence from the grave memories of youth
the shattering calamity of aborted dreams
the frenetic quest after vanished oases

Let yesterday sit in a dim restive chair
today, the bird awakes
in search of its lost migratory route.

2.
DARKNESS unveils the sword's aid
- a shimmering lesson –
concealed in the soul of the oak
a wingless acorn

autumn
and a pool of leaves erodes the earth
plumes into fresh foliage at spring

I AM there in the clipped
cloth of the bat
there in the damp hang-over

where a dream
must hatch in the whorl
of ash-ridden bones

DARKNESS
and the sword's whet point
spites the flesh of a new-winged bird.

3.
SUDDENLY
you find birthmarks in your scalp
knife-marks scar the face's angry mask

your frail screams
resound weirdly in the tumid skin
of the air

who is listening to a wingless bird
to the anguish of a frozen
podling?

the poet must hide
in the skin of the onion: a fugitive
fleeing

the rapid dragnet
of a fearsome flood.

4.
HAVING seen my own nakedness
suckled on the oak's rancid juice

I can now take down my goitre
from the sultry shelves
pluck my songs from rainstorm

hidden in the onion-skin
I can elongate into the soil
tuber into fibrous roots

in search
of the bird's buried plumes.

5.
AFRAID of the antique silence
of the oak
poet, you must recede into the smug
anonymity of the guild
compress in your tribe's memory
the blood-hardened communion of youth

your pursuers have gone up the hills
there they have erected their
multiple tents of torture
there to put on Dutch auction
the hardy plumes of the forge

man of the despoiled past
you who must weave from the thread
of raffia the messy matrix
of your tribe's soul
ascend the hills in your proof of words

ascend, o questioner
in your armour of Night's iron dungarees
let it shrink at the twitch of rain
- earth's garment of dearth –

RAINWASHED
the close-cropped scalp moults into foliage.

POEMS FOR CALICO, THE DUSTMAN OF SABO

1.
He was sitting there alone and sad
despising
the water's smooth surface
the bird's unruffled wing

he was in a tunnel lit
by an incomprehensible shaft
of darkness, seeing through mists
the eyeless dreams of youth

No one can set him free
of the chainmail of Time
the slow ceaselessly tapping rhythm

of a small stream emptying
into a drain

He was sitting there, just sitting there
alone and sad.

2.
There is that darkness in your eyes
it smoulders all prints of hope
bled from rock-white, from chalk and clay
your blood
flows freely into tunnels of waste

your sadness
- where is its source? –
its arms like arteries of the delta meeting
in the rapid vortex of your dis-
integrating selves

like arteries of death
the darkness in your eye illumines
the grey mystery of Time, plucks
from earth-wombs smitten roots
to scorn the mildewed feast

of dusk.

3.
You must meet the reaper's scythe
midway
bearing in your mildewed hands
the pickled chaff of memory

The sun has emerged beyond the ruffled
panes of dawn
following the footsteps of dew
across the lawn

Moistened in the dry sacs
of the corn, wait
prepare the path for the forger's knife
shake from bird-dust

The fragile strains of self.

4.
YOU must purge yourself
of your cant

amidst cindered roots find
the dark welt of your
impurity

lamp impales evening shadows
upon points of flame
hang

the damp overcoat
of your threnodic self: rive
the sweltering mast

of a floundering bark.

FOR CHIEF M.A. FABUNMI

1.
BRING your horns from the ancient rafters
bard
let us sing together a joint
salutation to the voices

beyond the gulf

in transit
I lost my tribal memory
abandoned in my unwieldy luggage
at the airport

bard, teach me anew
the forensic tale of the gods
the gnomic keys

of the ancient duet.

2.
FOLD me in your washcloth
of mystery: exile from bird-country

I carry my diplomatic pass
in the goitre of my neck:
searching through Time's immunity
the papered solemnity

of the bird in the fable –

Oh, bird on clothesline
if in flight you meet the fatal flint
turn, bird, turn
your breastplate of washcloth.

3.
Oh, grey mists accompanying sudden daybreak!
glimmerings pierce the ancient ash-cloth
of Night
in the sky, an invisible hand clears the smog
of dreams and Night's heraldry
trumpets from ancient rooftops

Ah, Papa!
mid-air – see!

Song-silvered plumes of a bird in flight.

*(Notes: Chief Michael Ajayi Fabunmi, 3ʳᵈ January 1906 –
May, 1990, was the foremost erudite high chief in Ile-Ife
when I was growing up. In this poem, I am a sapling
leaning on an ancient oak.)*

FAR FROM MY ERRANT SELVES

1.
I dread these moments of solitude
the horror in the wings of air

what breathes
in the antennae of Night –

the wild guts of vindictive
yesteryears?

2.
FAR from my errant selves
I find from wind-wash, surf

for my draughty faith
like a priest, leaning on the myth

of my calling; hands of dew
retract from hearthstones
gall stones of forbidden rituals

I walked these passages once
the sequestered caterpillar in broken
pupillage
the unravelling maze of dreams
in cocoons filled with cataracts

above the hooded pines, my voice
in a song of its own
REBIRTH.

3.
Yet these fears, the insomnia
in the cloth of dusk

peace cries rend the air but
what horrors people my suffering soul!

Night,
mortify my flesh, snarl its sinews
in your windless guts: ravel

my soul, let it decompose
in your moisty arms; drill

my bones, invade the very marrow
of my horrors!

NIGHT.

I PRESS FROM LEAF AND JUICE

I sap my flesh, still, seeking
the ultimate estrangement of flesh
and soul; perhaps

freed from its flesh, my soul
will ascend into the grey regions
of faith, wean from astral

mysteries the esoteric genes of its own
destruction; or, perhaps
freed from its soul

my flesh will revert to its cannibal
state, plumb beneath grey matter
into horizons of darkness, extort

from furtive glands
the salty rheum of a decomposing self

in this long-standing event
of soul combatting flesh and flesh
combatting soul, I retreat

into mists: I press from leaf and juice
new myths of earth; from molten dews

patent rites of being.

AMNESTY

We want amnesty for all political prisoners
For outside the sour scowl of iron-walls
Outside the hard-hitting rattling laws
Their anguish screams into our peace
The torment they face
- the torture that grinds into their flesh -
Fouls the serenity of our cities

Of what use are these slaughter-houses:
The gas chamber and its arsenic rites
The gallows and the monstrous callipers
The execution terraces ladened with birds of prey –
Of what use are these charnel-palaces
Whitewashed in the statutes of State?

We all want amnesty for prisoners
Of conscience; freedom from the gaoler's
Irate whims; freedom from the licenced lathes
Freedom from wanton crimes; from the firm darkness
Invading from the hills
We are Earth's children

The plumes that must ripen by Dusk.

SONG

Song comes from the dusty panes
of dusk – fragile willows
upon reedy banks

I trace in misty spaces
refrains of rain
piercing cries

from the rent wombs
of daybreak. I AM song
from the morning's very funnel

pouring votive hymns unto Earth.

ISAAC
(in memoriam)

1.
The pall breaks upon your song
ravels its feelers into alien codes

you are within the smitten code
the cutworm shrinking
into cyst

peering beneath the rim of leaf
dew-stained eyes

Of dusk.

2.
Farewell, Isaac
On your pilgrimage to the wilderness of Silence
To the under-streams of Time
Farewell to the dead march of drought
The dearth of lore in Night's dusky roof

Pilgrim shrouded in ancient fog
Shrug, Isaac, shrug off the latency of flesh
Conceal your soul in the tooth's powdery ore
Pierce earth's enamel cloth
Like ears of lettuce in shards of frost
Lime your bones in earth's dusty kiln

Farewell, Isaac
To the iron rites of the axe-guild
To life's lottery parlours, farewell
To forge-craft and flint-flares; the moist
Of rust glistening the womb at birth

Oh, farewell, Isaac!

(Notes: My uncle, Isaac, was a member of the Yoruba "Ogboni" fraternity, a true kind of masonic cult. I remember him fondly through my child's mind for the magical times of uncanny wizardry.)

OH, MAMMAN!

(in memory of Mamman Jiya Vatsa, executed March 5, 1986)

You have vanished too suddenly
like a vain swimmer on the crest of the tide
leaving us bewildered on the shores

amidst our grief-storm
the barren podling of our songs
the unpeopled dreams, the migrant faiths
shall we seek in seashells the season's futile angst
seek in the conches of forlorn years
the granite brows of communal gods?

FROM the pastures of Abuja
to the sombre irreality of Kirikiri
Mamman Jiya Vatsa lost out in a battle of wits
surprised the world not with a smile
but with a plot
not with pidgin poems and college rhymes
but with the promise of martial songs
the ricocheting threnody of a wakeful armoury

Perhaps, he was Plato in search
of an ideal Republic; perhaps, a Socrates
in tragic defence of logic
perhaps, even a Gaha, a monstrous
reformer of hidebound order
MJV, soldier, true to the end
you have vanished too suddenly

LIKE matchflare in wet breeze
or a paper kite in wind-wash
like the failing gleam of late dusk
the soldier-poet confronted his end
in the noose of State

SHOT, like a felon behind Ribadu Road.

IN MEMORY OF DELE GIWA

(murdered Sunday 19th of October 1986)

1.
The curtains hang drably
iron dress heavy on a weary audience…

the farce is over, the murder is done
the world hears nothing else
only the ruinous blast
of a parcel bomb.

2.
AND everywhere the shrapnel finds us still
beyond the school walls into the dark-
grimed streets; lingering long
the dying wail of the winds
the harsh feast of cindered songs

the immature twilight is here
cultured in this cesspool of darkness
the acrid aroma of blood-stained wine
the tragic frolic in midnight rites

paned: we listen to the rash chatter
of sudden shuttered windows…

3.
NIGHT, and we are earth's wanted felons
whence lonely shadows lean on life's lamp-posts

from muted dusk, from the anonymity
of grey-spectre mists
the hands of an unjust, inhuman society
knife us in the back

impale us on vain fortuitous crosses.

4.
THE centurion's point smites our flesh

leavened in Caesar's lewd fortune
in the venom of a cruel hierarchy

Caesar's men with wanton money
raid the fortress of our finest feelings
dispossess us of merely

THE malice and materiality
of our long-horned dreams.

ADIEU, Dele Giwa
adieu, gallant columnist
vanguard officer of the press corps

newsliner who takes his exit
in a rare whirlpool of words
find in this

music to refresh the flint
of your daring soul.

FOR SAMORA MACHEL

Even
If your plane crashes ten thousand times over
And you die so many times
The necessity of our revolution
Wakes us anew every time

- The iron thrall of apartheid South Africa
The plundering apparatus in Namibia
The deathly conspiracies of silence by the West –
They harden the fibre of our defiance

Fortified by your fearless feat
The fearless feat of a fighting people
Fortified by your heroic & exemplary death
The heroic & exemplary disposition of our people
We brace the barricade with our weapons
And trench the fortress to crush the enemy

CERTAINLY, in our struggle is victory
Adieu, Sam
Welcome, SAM!

I PROWL THE UNDERSTREAMS OF NIGHT

(Existential hymns to Night)

1.
Tonight, beneath the elms
I weigh my life sadly in the charred leaves
Of autumn, I weigh it piece-by-piece
In deep melancholy

What has happened beyond the horrible brow
Of sunlight, below the mangled gates
Of birth? Startled

By earth's infirmity, O poet
Recoil into the mystic rites
Of death, the purgatory roots
In Night's labyrinth of dream!

2.
You who gnash upon the surplice of Death
Carry away from me the dis-
Embowelled prophecy of being

O priests of the pumice stone, pierce me
Beneath the dark scarification
Beneath the tattooed fawn of dawn

Carry me away, away, away
Carry me far away to the land of Silence
The deep wilderness of being

Night, and the tale is stale
The venerable mask spins briskly, descends
Into the fog below

What missive you have from Adamu
Keep it close, O guardian
Keep it close to your tattooed nipples

Like sour breadfruit from alien screen!

3.
Memories plague the stillborn dusk
the half-bred hearth of dreams
the mists welcome you, stranger, thrash
in your mildewed eyes
the innocent harvest of earth

O stranger, followed by the fearful footfalls of Time
plunge beneath the ancient pyramids
prospect for the pumice stone
in the cavernous silence

Of Night.

4.
Listen, mask
Listen to the painful breath of the cowhide

Immigrant from far away, from the land
Of scrub, the enamel cloth of Earth
Whence these margins of drought
The empty rainstorms from Sky's anguished breasts?

I listen and I listen
And I keep pouring upon blank tablets
The faltering word of Death's high priest

Migrant self, fleeing the site of its own rust
Keep within the carapace of darkness
The half-chewed vitals of your own being
In Night's offertory box, your half-body

Keep, oh keep within the grey whorl of incense
The impotent latency of your phallic brand.

5.
I prowl the understreams of Night
the margins of listless silhouettes
from the coffers of mist, a thousand footsteps
chortling down a hollow chimney

Whence these wakeful voices in the spine of walls
the shadows etched on frames of flame
the myth indented like incisions
in the scalp of Night

O the plague of memories
this threnody of a half-child – alone –
in the sheepskin of birth
this augury in a furious sky -

Death's mask upon the misted molten brow
of a devastated god!

MASKS

1.
You who prowl the interior silence of Night
for you this ancient hymn

Mask of death beneath the cloudface
of Night; long feelers of bone, gnawing
into the anthill flesh of Night

You who thread the interior loom of Earth
yarns of Death in the cellars beneath
Night's own shrouded myths

I conjure you as surrogate
in my alchemic rites

wipe from my soul the grave mist
of age, wean
from the interior echoes of my passing voice
new hymns of birth; halt

me in my pilgrimage to the far depths
to the deep ancestry of my soul; oh
Mask of death, lama in the lantern
of a lambent mystery –

Conjoin in your gnarled veins
the veins of your rancid roots
the roots of your ponderous hands
of Fate, conjoin me

in your desecrated mysteries, free me
from the onrush of rust; from the decay
of the tortoise's shell; from the detached
quill, lifeless in Night's

fortune tray: let the wind
recompose my breath; let me flow
free with the upward draught
bud – from nursery –

in the nipples of Earth, let
anguished semes of self burst
the mystery of being:
OH, mask!

2.
YOU who hang upon my brow
the desultory shrouds of dusk: remove
from your dirge its paternal cadence
from my breathless form, remove

your curb of death;
I AM forge-flame, the kindred gene
of iron kernels, I AM kite-beak
the vulture's ominous talons
I AM adamant feathers flung earthwards
I AM steel-wings, outstretched
in mockery of dusk, I AM rock
- terra firma –

in vain your curb of death
the cadenced rancour of tumoured winds
the airless vision in Night's ancient pyjamas
I AM earth

- terra firma –

3.
WHY must I succumb to the instincts
of flesh? Oh, hear,
my own flesh is armoured against its own soul
my flesh wants to secede in the far depths
of Night's anthill flesh

my flesh wants to go and dwell
in the airless corridors of Night; my flesh
wants to suckle the rasping silence
of Night, Night's mysterious froth of stillness

Oh, rebel, master plotter, ingrate
are these my proper deserts
for those years of slow laborious love
for living like a vulture

on account of your innumerable appetites
is this how you must bring to nought
my seasons of abstinence
my diet on seashells, quills and rain-juice
on turtles, beetles and weevils?

Oh, SOUL, fortify all your ramparts
invade the fortress of flesh
with your ballistic tensions; sack
the vain strongholds with forge-flame

grind iron kernels in flesh's rancid scalp
break kite-beak like bitumen
like the vulture's ominous talon
in flesh's courtyard of irate limbs

grow adamant feathers
in the threshold of flesh; people
its proud churchyard with steel-wings
in mockery of dusk; comb
with granite, the hardware of mutinous cells

Oh, SOUL, overrun the epicentre of flesh
cut it into dominions; submerge it whole
in your own evanescent centrifugal force
claim it in the ravelling myth of foregone essence

Oh, flesh!

THE HOUSE OF AGELESS NOD

For those who want the exactitude
Of death, o, find parallel
Of the ageless nod in Night's antique repose

Beneath the date palm, there's your mound
Your life in Earth's compost pit
Foul your nostrils – brother –
With the breath of maggots; incline

Your skull in the sofa of slime
Let your eyes flow
Like rheum into the tiny holes
Of the artisan's skill, pull

From roots, the gangrene of flesh
Of sinews seeping beneath the pall
In the fabric of the shroud
Searching for missing fingers and toes

Oh, brother of the eyeless skull
Prince of the house of ageless nod
A-tune hymns to Death's organ recital
Bate your breath and tell the grave-digger:

You too, friend, will pass on
Like instinctive birds across the gulf
Of seas; or rain reeling

Into Earth, or ancient blade bled
From grey parent at the touch of breeze
Oh, friend, you too will pass on
Into the midst of ageless dusk

You must listen for the cockerel's thunder
At dusk, hear it, briefly, the march of mists
Behind the cockerel's comb, see, approaching
The silent hooves of the horseman's herald
The rasp of raffia rattling at the rim
The hush of Earth, of vast portals
Hung at berth for Earth's anchoring vessel

At dusk, hear it, briefly, friend
Hear it, briefly, and lapse
Into the raw rhythm of somnolent
Earth; pass on beyond the raffia of dream
Beyond the cysts of mists – the grey
Womb of birth – beyond beyond

Pass on, friend – grave-digger, teacher
Philosopher, king, pass on, friend
Pass on into the artifice
Of ageless nod.

PORCELAIN

Petal of dark gold

I have plucked from the stalk
Of dew
The very beginning

Dawn loner to the font
I have lapped on icy purity
The friendly corrosion in the belly of the horn

She
My dark gold – luminous, pure
Translucent, soft, fluorescent

I hold in the shelves of my heart
A hoard of herbs
Deep in the earth of my dreams
A porcelain of yeast leavens.

FAR AWAY FROM YOU

1.
FAR away from you
the dark patience in your eyes comes across
the pounding ferocity of highlife tunes

I withdraw from the crowds
drawn into the magic rhythm of our lives
desire wells up in me

to think of your soft girlish giggles

my love
even here, I feel the tyranny of distance –
so withdrawn

into the numbing cyst
of homesickness.

2.
DARKNESS clothes the evening mist
but not the memories we share together

in the counterpane of Time
long rolls of laughter clasp at the waistline
thus yoked

we dance to the midrib
of the tide, I see

from the crest of the arc
two souls, hand-in-hand, trudging

down an empty valley
to the sunshine beyond.

3.
BELOVED
I want to sing your name on the reed pines
catch in the breath of the wind
the long fragrance of your presence

hidden in the tall ferns
listen to my whistle break the curtain
of the dusk, listen
to the calm rhapsody of my wind instruments

girl of my dream
shared from the fertile passion of my youth
it is your name that emblazons the olden altars
your name, the signature of a world re-made:

love-drunk
this poem becomes a vow
this song a psalm.

4.
ALONE in the night, naked
and on my back
I squirm in the loneliness
of the vast hall, tormented

by your nude apparition
and my own marauding passion

mermaid
if this be love, I must submit like elf
before the tide, and dance, navel to navel

to a long-desired climax

Night.

PLUCK ME LIKE LEAF

1.
Your flesh troubles my soul, grinds
Into the secret crop of a desolate
Earth: how I wish I was there – naked –
Amidst the storm, surf travelling
Through the sea's swollen stride

Your flesh troubles my soul, grates
Into the nape of dream, the foul
Collar beneath Night's dusty jacket; clad
In the sultry pyjamas of earth
Sky's ancient heir

Wrings his empty hands into opening leaves:
Like sentry or chaperon, please
Lonely one, divest me of dusk clothes
Of the swivelling clads of natal air; prime
Me like earth

For rain gathered in the brow
Of the trembling leaf
Free of the millstone of dusk
Pagan, I must restore to Earth's own
Womb, the ritual promise of rust.

2.
I watch you between the dark surplices
Of Night; flesh apart from soul, limp
In the embrace of Night's brutal tranquil

I watch your soul hang
In the curtains at sunset, like a slender yarn
In the spider's loom. Far

From the censer of your own life
How can I, lonely one, un-cleave
The ribs of mist, hazard, like Sango

The sundering of ancient gates
With thundering songs? O, lonely one
Disinvest me of my counterweights

My dishonoured checks like
Awful balance at the grocer's stall; disinvest
Me of rain's harsh communion

Sunburst – I search amidst stardust
Pollens for my new-found
Rite.

3.
Help me to grow, please
To your God – blue eyes in the white
Counterpane of rust – your God
Sundered into three for the sake of love

Sundered into magic rites
On a cross, purge me of dross
Of Night's blunderbuss, teach me
The rite of flesh and blood

I am animist, earth's totem
Of ripening corn, shear me of lorn plumes
Of the cob's mane of rust, teach me
The glossary of your font

Help me to love, please
Lonely one, help me to grow across the counterpane
Of dust, brown eyes in place of white
Initiate me into the soul's own cult

To counter the rush of Death; pluck
Me like leaf from the sea's
Swollen pride, like lettuce
From the lingering peril of storm

O, lovely one!

SONG OF THE WAISTRUFF

INTACT within your flesh
I re-enact my rite of being: the dreams
I have wasted in Time's
frugal thirst

BELOVED
I am dry to the bones, dry
beyond the loins where
mat unravels the complex portents

ON the waistruff, I want your songs
anew, the liqueur you strain
from the empty dusk; I

WANT to lie intact in your skin
travel like breath
to the far corridors of your soul

I AM dry to the bones, dry
below the navel, below the tattoos
of birth. Night unfurls

LIKE an arc
upon the roofs of ancient myths
like broken bark for myriad taboos

DANCE, beloved
wake the dusk with the rustling
of your waistruff, conceal

ME from lingering thirst
from Time's taboos and myths
naked like the full-orbed moon, Earth's offspring

PRINT upon Night's prayer wheel
Their own existential songs.

AFTERWARDS

1.
IN your presence, I slough off my self-waste
the grey sterility of my soul
flare from the white ash of my youth
your eyes unveil the moments of my life
ignite my sodden splint

torched
I crackle with warmth, tar
wending down the long neck
of my oil-lamp

girl
you cannot imagine the quickening
passion
with which you inflame me
nor can this simple poem recall
the willing crouch
my love-ladened being must make…

night
hallowed by silence and darkness
I am the sparkling star campaigning
for the silky hands of the moon

love-drunk
I must weave through dark runnels
to the breast of the fount
un-bidden.

2.
magical
the night wraps us in its fold
of silence

we listen to the hushed songs
of insects in the grass
fashioning

from crickets' cries
the twittering harmony of our own lives

what can I say after that fierce contest
of flesh on flesh
after the eruptive season of our love –

that I hear nothing of the whipping winds
that below the coverlet, we mould from sweat
fresh oaths of love?

Slack in the warm welcome of your arms
I confess myself a novice
in this forge of magic and rapture.

3.
AFTERWARDS…

I drill from the cellar of the night
rich wine of youth

from the somnolent slogans of fireflies
new malt to nurture
a world re-made

afterwards…
cool, calm, renewed
ripe rain in drought.

NEW YEAR'S EVE SLEUTH

1.
ABOUT us
the shards of a passing year
the weary voices of ancient seasons

grey in the limping harmattan
a ceremonial mask ascending
into fog

the market vanishes rapidly
its swarms flee into nightfall
earth's draughty stalls

peopled with mildewed moths.

2.
VANQUISHED:
a year gathers moss in the plain
anterooms – unfurling

the canvas of a coming year

bold, even in the encroaching
darkness, the half-size
imprints of a bygone prince

passing prince, your kingdom is eroded
new men emerge from the ribs
of dusk, they bear in fragile veins

leaves of coming seasons, like cryptic scrolls
they trail wet roots across the smoggy lawn
to lick from dew the strange tolls of dawn.

3.
I kept my vigil well
and saw in ebbing mist
the outflowing tide of a passing year

below the rim of the roofs
old dreams stretching their withering hands
half-clothed shadows, limping
into the drumskin of fog

ahead in a dosshouse
an old year tends the final flickering flame
at the belfry, slow lingering echoes
sky-blown, happy fragments of broken china

daybreak, and the new year is here
a crouching fellow with sunlight
to christen his balding pate

I saw him climb the thistled
staff of the advent sun, Time's
frost-funnelled flywhisk hanging –

like an old almanac
from the graven sleeves of his ceremonial robes.

THE POET'S CALL

it was you who called
Moriama
silent woman of the ancient kraal
captured in the bowels of night

I caught
the solemn tone of your incantation
the oracular passion
of your dark songs

woman of misery
you who knead from the sweat
of your long servitude
several wet peens of hope

woman of the forgotten mountains
whose eyes are full
of broken dreams
whose back runs with natal scars

Moriama
daughter of the bull
daughter of the ancient matador
daughter of fallen heroes led away at nightfall
to alien slaughterhouses by tribal chieftains

it was you who called
Moriama
and I listened across the tinge

of dry tobacco leaves
I heard the rasp breath of the totem snake
slithering down the wattle clothed in dung
I heard you - beyond the muffled cacophony
of ancient griots, far from the mournful songs
of my youth!

I caught my name anew
nymph
roused from the brown dust
of the ancient ruins
wet wings roused from sleep

NOW
I must learn to stand the chill
of the harmattan
learn to live the promise
of a long-awaited apocalypse.

I ANOINT MY EYES

It is a season of masks
We must bleed from raffia
The ancient cult-word
To transmute the plainness of the age

I anoint my eyes
Upon Night's own counterpane
I plumb like tender feelers
Into Time's arcane anterooms

I anoint my ears
Let the password recede into the flesh
Of my being – dissolve in its profanity
The tumoured breast of rain

I plumb earth's fragile lap
Like greying leaf
I break from two single halves
New sheaves of selves

I anoint my flesh
In Night's dusk-templed font
Let it decompose in its tweeds of rust
Mount into plumes of flint

O mask of a disappearing Night
From all sources of paraffin
Withdraw: lest a-flamed
You torch with your branch

The splint of your own being!

POSTSCRIPT

*(for Captain Thomas Sankara, deposed in a bloody
coup, October 15, 1987)*

Like a cameleer from a desert sojourn
He sought to pinch from drought
Moist to cross the thirst
Of leaf – distraught with dust –

He sought clues
Of dew, frail moisture from inert
Manure; fraught with reins of rust –
He wrought in iron the craft of State: Thomas

You who wrung from the wrath of the West
Leafage of a new lease of life
You who spurned the sovereignty of office
And camped at the bottom of the valley

Poor Christ of Ouagadougou, lynched
By his own mob, his ashes – like a popular leaflet –
Flung across the compass of history
Captain Thomas Sankara

Salute to your youthful heroic soul!